A Stained Glass C with Heavenly Carols

Alfred Publishing Co., Inc.
16320 Roscoe Blvd., Suite 100
P.O. Box 10003
Van Nuys, CA 91410-0003
alfred.com

To order this DVD and HD DVD featuring this great Christmas music in stereo and 5.1 Surround Sound along with stunning Christmas scenes in stained glass, vist www.concerthotspot.com

ISBN-10: 0-7390-4901-1
ISBN-13: 978-0-7390-4901-3

CONTENTS

SILENT NIGHT

Words and Music by
JOSEPH MOHR
and FRANZ GRUBER

Silent Night, Holy Night, All is calm, all is bright, round yon virgin Mother and child. Holy infant so tender and mild. Sleep in heavenly

Silent Night - 3 - 1

4

JOY TO THE WORLD

Words by
ISAAC WATTS

Music by
GEORGE F. HANDEL

Joy to the World - 2 - 1

THE FIRST NOËL

Traditional

Moderately slow

1. The first Noel the angel did say, Was to cer-tain poor shep-herds in fields as they lay; In fields where they lay keep-ing their sheep On a cold win-ter's night that was so deep.

Refrain

No - el, No - el, No - el, No - el,

Born is the King of Is - ra - el.

HARK! THE HERALD ANGELS SING

Words by
CHARLES WESLEY

Music by
FELIX MENDELSSOHN

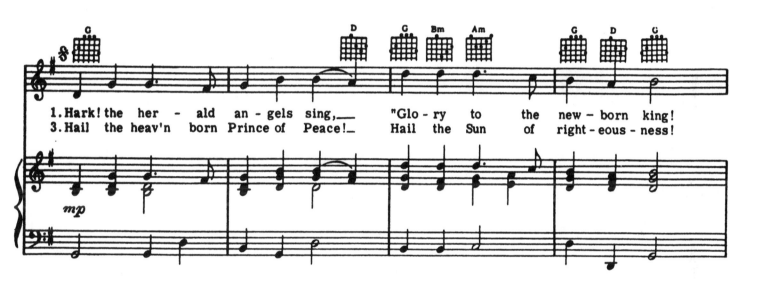

1. Hark! the her - ald an - gels sing,___ "Glo - ry to the new - born king!
3. Hail the heav'n born Prince of Peace!___ Hail the Sun of right - eous - ness!

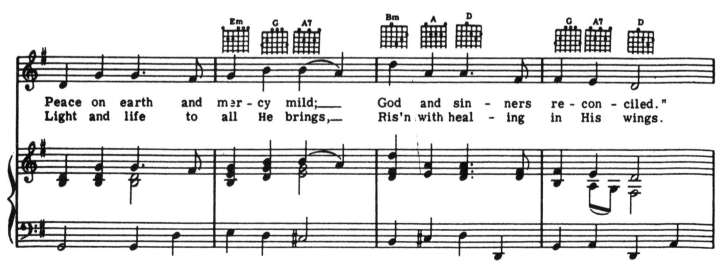

Peace on earth and mer - cy mild;___ God and sin - ners re - con - ciled."
Light and life to all He brings,___ Ris'n with heal - ing in His wings.

Hark! The Herald Angels Sing - 3 - 1

O COME, ALL YE FAITHFUL

(Adeste Fideles)

English Words by FREDERICK OAKELEY
Latin Words Attributed to JOHN FRANCIS WADE

Music by
JOHN READING

2. Sing, choirs of angels,
   Sing in exultation,
   Sing, all ye citizens of heaven above:
   Glory to God
   In the highest glory!
   O come, let us adore Him, etc.

3. Yea, Lord, we greet Thee,
   Born this happy morning,
   Jesus, to Thee be glory giv'n,
   Word of the Father,
   Now in flesh appearing.
   O come, let us adore Him, etc.

✓ MARY HAD A BABY

Traditional

Moderately

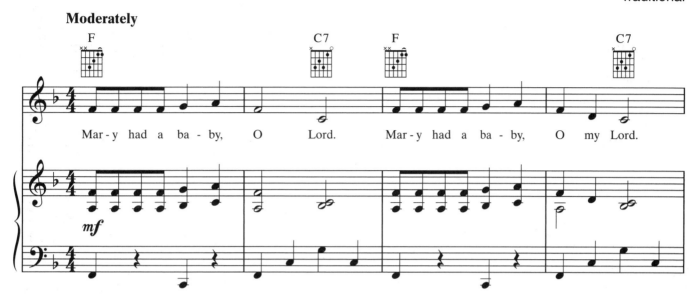

Mar-y had a ba-by, O Lord. Mar-y had a ba-by, O my Lord.

Mar-y had a ba-by, O Lord. The peo-ple keep a-com-ing and the train done gone.

AWAY IN A MANGER

Words by
MARTIN LUTHER

Music by
JONATHAN E. SPILLMAN

A - way in a__ man - ger, no crib for His bed, The
Be near me, Lord__ Je - sus, I ask Thee to stay

lit - tle Lord Je - sus lay down His sweet head. The
by me for - ev - er and love me I pray. Bless

stars in the__ heav - ens looked down where He lay, The
all the dear__ chil - dren in Thy where ten - der care And

lit - tle Lord Je - sus a - sleep in the hay. The__
take us to Heav - en to live with Thee there. A -

Away in a Manger - 2 - 1

JESU, JOY OF MAN'S DESIRING

JOHANN SEBASTIAN BACH

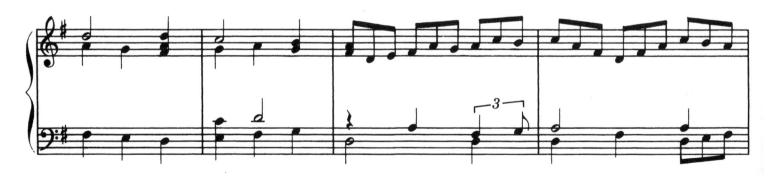

Jesu, Joy of Man's Desiring - 4 - 1

18

rit.

SANS DAY CAROL

Traditional

BRING A TORCH, JEANNETTE, ISABELLA

Traditional

I SAW THREE SHIPS

Traditional English

Verse 6:
And all the bells on earth shall sing
On Christmas Day, On Christmas Day.
And all the bells on earth shall sing
On Christmas Day in the morning.

Verse 7:
And all the Angels in heaven shall sing
On Christmas Day, On Christmas Day.
And all the Angels in heaven shall sing
On Christmas Day in the morning.

Verse 8:
And all the souls on earth shall sing
On Christmas Day, On Christmas Day.
And all the souls on earth shall sing
On Christmas Day in the morning.

Verse 9:
Then let us all rejoice, amain,
On Christmas Day, On Christmas Day.
Then let us all rejoice, amain,
On Christmas Day in the morning

O HOLY NIGHT
(Cantique de Noel)

By
ADOLPHE CHARLES ADAM

O ho - ly night! The stars are bright - ly shin - ing. It is the
night of our dear Sav - iour's birth. Long lay the world in sin and er - ror
pin - ing, till He ap-pear'd and the soul felt its worth, A thrill of hope the

O Holy Night - 2 - 1

UNTO US IS BORN A SON

Traditional

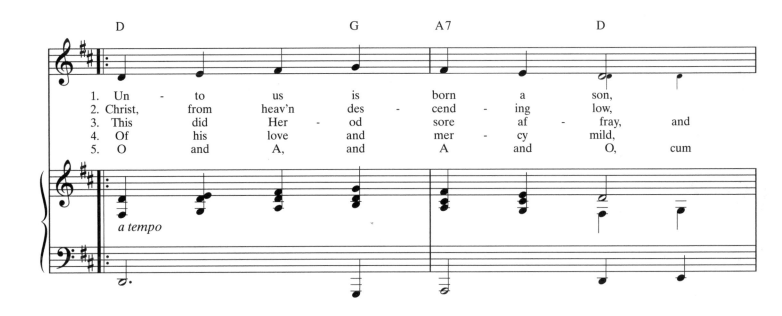

1. Un - to us is born a son,
2. Christ, from us heav'n des - cend - ing low,
3. This did Her - od sore af - fray, and
4. Of his love and mer - cy mild,
5. O and A, and A and O, cum

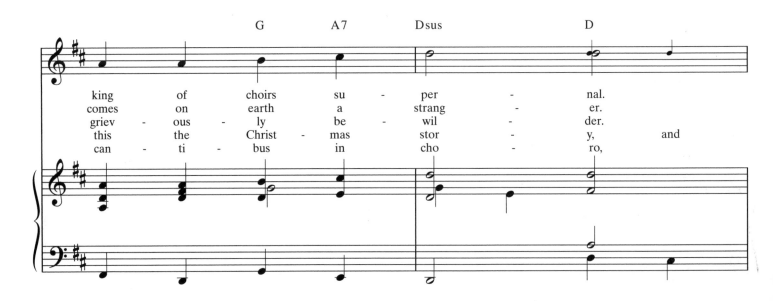

king of choirs su - per - nal.
comes on earth a strang - er.
griev - ous - ly be - wil - der.
this the Christ - mas stor - y, and
can - ti - bus in cho - ro,

Unto Us Is Born a Son - 2 - 1

GOOD KING WENCESLAS

Words by
JOHN MASON NEALE

Traditional English Carol

2. "Hither, page, and stand by me,
If thou know'st it telling,
Yonder peasant, who is he?
Where and what his dwelling?"
"Sire, he lives a good league hence,
Underneath the mountain,
Right against the forest fence,
By St. Agnes' fountain."

3. "Bring me flesh, and bring me wine,
Bring me pine logs hither;
Thou and I will see him dine,
When we bear them thither."
Page and monarch, forth they went,
Forth they went together;
Through the rude wind's wild lament,
And the bitter weather.

4. "Sire, the night is darker now,
And the wind blows stronger;
Fails my heart, I know not how;
I can go no longer."
"Mark my footsteps my good page,
Tread thou in them boldly:
Thou shalt find the winter's rage
Freeze thy blood less coldly."

5. In his master's steps he trod,
Where the snow lay dinted;
Heat was in the very sod
Which the Saint had printed.
Therefore, Christian men, be sure,
Wealth or rank possessing,
Ye who now will bless the poor,
Shall yourselves find blessing.

AVE MARIA

FRANZ SCHUBERT, Op. 52

Ave Maria - 9 - 1

NATIVITY CAROL

Traditional
Arranged by JOHN RUTTER

Andante tranquillo ♩ = 100

Nativity Carol - 2 - 1

IN DULCI JUBILO
(Christ Was Born For This)

Traditional

FOR UNTO US A CHILD IS BORN

(from "The Messiah")

By GEORGE FRIDERIC HANDEL

For Unto Us a Child Is Born - 9 - 1

42

For Unto Us a Child Is Born - 9 - 2

48

the might - y God, the ev - er - last - ing Fa - ther, the

Prince of Peace, the ev - er - last - ing Fa - ther, the Prince of Peace.

For Unto Us a Child Is Born - 9 - 9

O COME, O COME, EMMANUEL

Traditional

O Come, O Come, Emmanuel - 2 - 2

O LITTLE TOWN OF BETHLEHEM

PHILLIPS BROOKS

LEWIS H. REDNER

O Little Town of Bethlehem - 2 - 1

O Little Town of Bethlehem - 2 - 2

IT CAME UPON THE MIDNIGHT CLEAR

Words by
EDMUND H. SEARS

Music by
RICHARD S. WILLIS

It Came Upon the Midnight Clear - 2 - 1

3. And ye beneath life's crushing load,
   Whose forms are bending low,
   Who toil along the climbing way
   With painful steps and slow,
   Look now! for glad and golden hours
   Come swiftly on the wing.
   O rest beside the weary road
   And hear the angels sing.

4. For lo, the days are hast'ning on,
   By prophet bards foretold,
   When with the ever circling years
   Comes round the age of gold,
   When peace shall over all the earth
   Its ancient splendor fling,
   And the whole world give back the song
   Which now the angels sing.

HERE WE COME A-CAROLING
(The Wassail Song)

Old English

With spirit

Verse:

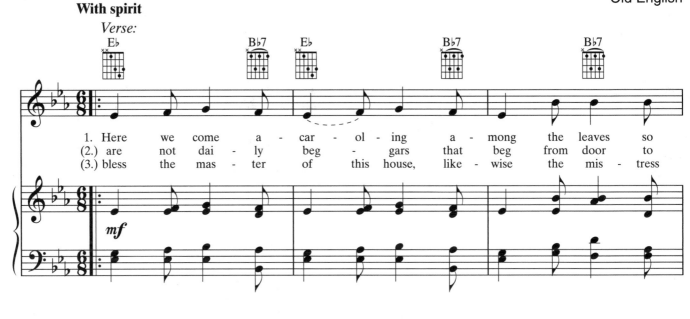

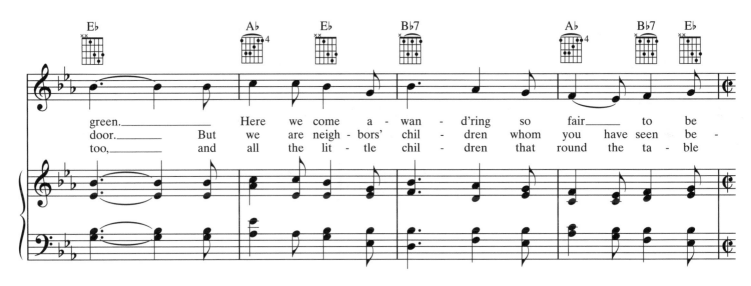

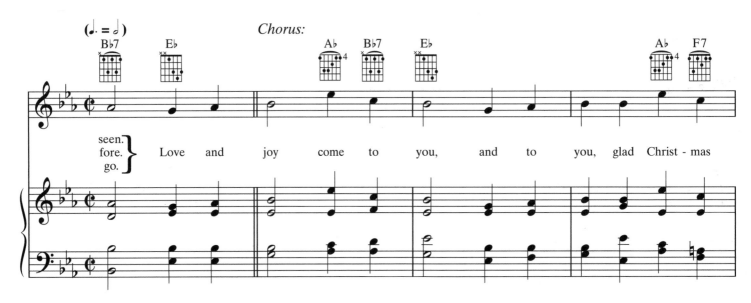

Here We Come A-Caroling - 2 - 1

GREENSLEEVES
(What Child Is This?)

By WILLIAM C. DIX
Old English Air

Gently

Verse:

1. What child is this___ who
lies He in___ such
bring Him in - cense,

(with pedal)

laid to rest,___ on Mar - y's lap___ is sleep - ing, whom an - gels great___ with
mean es - tate___ where ox and ass___ are feed - ing? Good Chris - tian, fear___ for
gold and myrrh.___ Come pea - sant king___ to own___ Him. The King of Kings___ sal -

an - thems sweet___ while shep - herds watch___ are keep - ing?
sin - ners here.___ The si - lent Word___ is plead - ing.
va - tion brings.___ Let lov - ing hearts___ en - throne Him.

GOD REST YE MERRY, GENTLEMEN

Traditional English Carol

God Rest Ye Merry, Gentlemen - 2 - 1

Refrain:

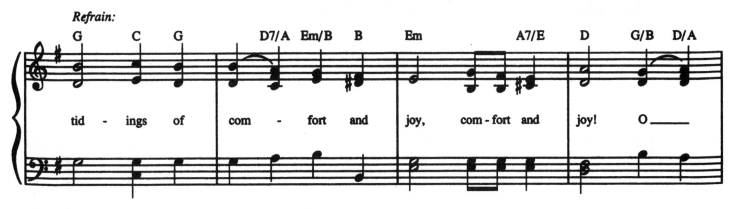

tid - ings of com - fort and joy, com - fort and joy! O _____

tid - ings of com - fort and joy! _____ 2. In joy!

Verse 3:
From God, our Heav'nly Father,
A blessed Angel came,
And unto certain Shepherds
Brought tidings of the same;
How that in Bethlehem was born
The Son of God by Name.
(To Refrain:)

Verse 4:
"Fear not, then," said the Angel,
"Let nothing you affright,
This day is born a Saviour,
Of a pure Virgin bright,
To free all those who trust in Him
From Satan's power and might."
(To Refrain:)

Verse 5:
The Shepherds at those tidings
Rejoiced much in mind;
And left their flocks a-feeding,
In tempest, storm and wind;
And went to Bethlehem straight-way,
The Son of God to find.
(To Refrain:)

Verse 6:
Now to the Lord sing praises,
All you within this place,
And with true love and brotherhood
Each other now embrace;
This holy tide of Christmas
All other doth deface.
(To Refrain:)

ANGELS WE HAVE HEARD ON HIGH

Traditional

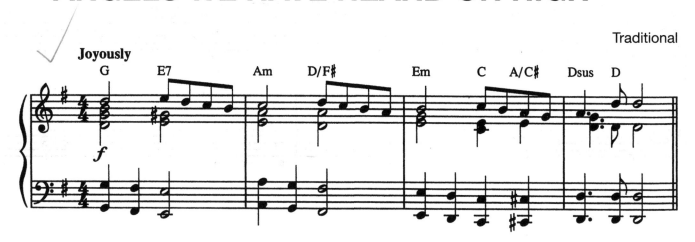

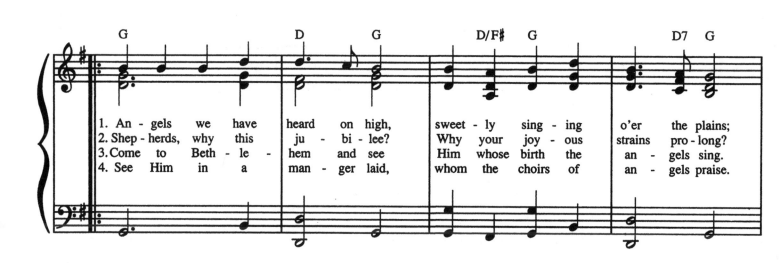

1. An - gels we have heard on high, sweet - ly sing - ing o'er the plains;
2. Shep - herds, why this ju - bi - lee? Why your joy - ous strains pro - long?
3. Come to Beth - le - hem and see Him whose birth the an - gels sing.
4. See Him in a man - ger laid, whom the choirs of an - gels praise.

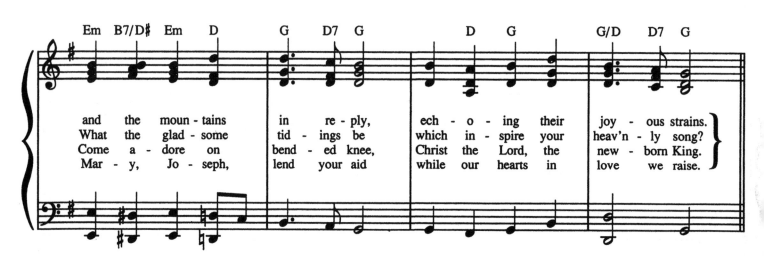

and the moun - tains in re - ply, ech - o - ing their joy - ous strains.
What the glad - some tid - ings be which in - spire your heav'n - ly song?
Come a - dore on bend - ed knee, Christ the Lord, the new - born King.
Mar - y, Jo - seph, lend your aid while our hearts in love we raise.

Angels We Have Heard on High - 2 - 1

HALLELUJAH! CHORUS
(from "The Messiah")

By GEORGE FRIDERIC HANDEL

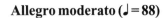

Allegro moderato (♩ = 88)

Hallelujah! Chorus - 8 - 1

71

Hallelujah! Chorus - 8 - 8

AND THE GLORY OF THE LORD

(from "The Messiah")

By GEORGE FRIDERIC HANDEL

Allegro

And the glo - ry, the glory of the Lord. And the glo - ry, the glory of the Lord shall be re -

And the Glory of the Lord - 6 - 1

And the Glory of the Lord - 6 - 2

74

shall be re - veal - ed, and all flesh___ shall

see___ it to - geth - er, to - geth - er. For the mouth of the

Lord___ hath spo - ken it, for the mouth of the

cresc.

Adagio
ff

Lord___ hath spo - ken it.

ff

the first christmas release in high definition HD DVD/S
plays on either HD DVD or standard DVD players!

A Stained Glass Christmas

with Heavenly Carols

plays on either HD DVD OR STANDARD DVD players!

This unprecedented Christmas release features high definitio
views of the world's most beautiful stained glass Nativity
artwork , holiday scenery and churches accompanied by mo
than 150 minutes of the season's most treasured Christmas
songs by choirs, symphonies, and soloists – all in Dolby Dig
5.1 Surround and shot in 1080i HD. This release features tw
soundtracks – one of 25 selected Christmas carols and the
other of highlights of Handel's Messiah.

With footage selected from magnificent landmark churches,
cathedrals, galleries and museums, A STAINED GLASS
CHRISTMAS WITH HEAVENLY CAROLS captures the opalescent
perfection of Louis Comfort Tiffany glass and John La Farge
glass as well as the stunning, world renowned works of artisa
studios in Munich, Chicago, Innsbruck, London and Venice.

SOUNDTRACK ONE:
CHRISTMAS CAROLS

Joy to the World

Silent Night

The First Noel

Hark! The Herald Angels Sing

O Come, All Ye Faithful

Away in a Manger

Bach - Jesu Joy of Man's Desiring

Sans Day Carol

Mary had a Baby

Bring a Torch Jenette & Isabella

O Holy Night

I Saw Three Ships

Unto Us Is Born A Son

Good King Wencelas

Nativity Carol

Schubert - Ave Maria

In Dulci Jubino
(Christ Was Born For This)

O Come, O Come Emmanuel

Oh Little Town of Bethlehem

It Came Upon a Midnight Clear

Here We Come a Caroling

Greensleeves (What Child is This

God Rest Ye Merry Gentlemen

Angels We Have Heard on High

SOUNDTRACK TWO:
HANDEL'S MESSIAH

Hallelujah! / Overture / Comfo
Ye / Every Valley / And the Glor
of the Lord / Thus Saith the Lor
of Hosts / But Who May Abide /
Behold! A Virgin Shall Conceiv
O Thou That Tellest Good
Tidings to Zion / He Shall Feed
His Flock / I Know that My
Redeemer Liveth / For Unto us
Child is Born / And Suddenly th
was With the Angel a Multitude
Glory to God / Rejoice Greatly,
O Daughter of Zion / His Yoke
Easy / Behold! The Lamb of Go
All We, Like Sheep / Hallelujah!
The Trumpet Shall Sound / Am

SELLING POINTS

* Available on HD DVD/Standard Def Hybrid
  disc (plays on both HD DVD player and
  standard DVD player)

* Press releases pushed to regional and national
  publications

* DVD will be featured by public television as
  a December Christmas special

concert
HOT
SPOT

Street Date: November 14, 2006

HD DVD/SD

SRP: HD DVD/SD: $29.99
GENRE: CHRISTMAS

8 90039 00111 2